On The Development Of The Flower Of Pinguicula Vulgaris

Alexander Dickson

In the interest of creating a more extensive selection of rare historical book reprints, we have chosen to reproduce this title even though it may possibly have occasional imperfections such as missing and blurred pages, missing text, poor pictures, markings, dark backgrounds and other reproduction issues beyond our control. Because this work is culturally important, we have made it available as a part of our commitment to protecting, preserving and promoting the world's literature. Thank you for your understanding.

*To Professor A. Gray M.D.
with the Author's Comp^{ts}*

ON THE

DEVELOPMENT

OF THE

FLOWER OF PINGUICULA VULGARIS, L.

WITH REMARKS ON THE

EMBRYOS OF P. VULGARIS, P. GRANDIFLORA, P. LUSITANICA,
P. CAUDATA, AND UTRICULARIA MINOR.

BY

ALEXANDER DICKSON, M.D., Edin. & Dublin.,
REGIUS PROFESSOR OF BOTANY IN THE UNIVERSITY OF GLASGOW.

FROM THE
TRANSACTIONS OF THE ROYAL SOCIETY OF EDINBURGH, Vol. XXV.

EDINBURGH:
PRINTED FOR THE SOCIETY BY NEILL AND COMPANY.
MDCCCLXIX.
1869

XVIII.—*On the Development of the Flower of* Pinguicula vulgaris, *L.; with Remarks on the Embryos of* P. vulgaris, P. grandiflora, P. lusitanica, P. caudata, *and* Utricularia minor. By ALEXANDER DICKSON, M.D. Edin. & Dublin.; Regius Professor of Botany in the University of Glasgow. (Plates XXVIII.-XXX.)

(Read 19th April 1869.)

The order Lentibulariaceæ is usually described in systematic works as exhibiting affinities, on the one hand with Scrophulariaceæ, which it resembles in the bilabiate corolla, partial suppression of the androecium, bilabiate stigma, and two-valved capsule; and, on the other, with Primulaceæ and its allies, with which it agrees in having a truly free central placenta.

LINDLEY places the order in his alliance of Bignoniales, along with Scrophulariaceæ, apparently following Mr BENTHAM, whom he quotes in support of the supposed affinity between the families.[*] Others, again, more impressed with the importance of the placental character, place the family near Primulaceæ, as has been done by PAYER.[†]

In the hope that the study of the development of the flower in Lentibulariaceæ might throw some light on the question of the affinities of the order, I have, from time to time during several years past, taken up the investigation of the organogeny of the flower of *Pinguicula vulgaris*, according as opportunities occurred for collecting suitable material; and I now venture to lay my results, imperfect as they still are, before this Society.

If a plant of *Pinguicula vulgaris* be examined during the flowering season, it is found to exhibit a short axis, on which are crowded a variable number of leaves, spreading out in a rosette-like manner upon the surface of the soil or turf on which the plant is found. This short axis is terminated by a contracted indefinite inflorescence, consisting of a variable number of ebracteate flowers with long pedicels—an unstalked umbel, in fact, analogous to that in the ordinary form of *Primula vulgaris*. Immediately below the inflorescence, a leaf-bud is found in the axil of the last leaf. As the fruit ripens, the leaves of the main axis gradually wither off, and the main axis itself decays; the original rosette becoming replaced in the autumn by a similar one, resulting from the development of the axillary bud of its last leaf. On the approach of winter, the

---

[*] Vegetable Kingdom, p. 686.   [†] Leçons sur les Fam. Nat. des Plantes, p. 14.

expanded outer leaves of the autumn rosette disappear; the central portion remaining as a firm, bulb-like, winter-resting bud, the outer leaves of which are developed as somewhat fleshy scales. This bulb-like bud remains during the winter sunk in the soil, or among the surrounding moss; and, on the return of warm weather the next season, expands into the summer-rosette, terminated by the inflorescence as above described.

Rudiment of the Inflorescence in Winter-Bud.

On removing the leaves from the winter-resting bud, the following structures appear:—1*st*, A cushion-like mass in the axil of the last leaf, the rudiment of the bud which developes the autumn-rosette of the next season, and becomes the flowering plant of the summer thereafter. This cushion usually (always?) appears somewhat depressed, in a direction corresponding to the middle line of the supporting leaf, as I have indicated in Plate XXVIII. fig. 1; but as to the significance of this median furrow, I am unable to offer any suggestion. 2*d*, The termination of the main axis, which appears as an unequally three-sided cushion, nearly flat on the top, and with rounded angles, the largest and thickest of which represents the rudiment of the first flower, the angle next in size representing that of the second flower, and the remaining angle (often very obscure) that of the third flower.

These floral rudiments continue, as to position, the spiral succession of the leaves upon the main axis. If a number of plants be examined, the spiral will be found running sometimes to the right, and sometimes to the left, in about equal proportions (see figs. 1, 2, 3, 4, 5, and 9). The fraction expressing the leaf-arrangement appears to be $\frac{5}{13}$ approximately; and the spiral succession of leaves developed upon the axillary shoot of the last leaf is homodromous with that of the main axis.

Early Obliquity of the Floral Axis.

Almost as soon as the young flower has begun distinctly to project from the axis of inflorescence, and before there is any appearance of sepals or other floral parts, it is seen to be more developed on the anterior aspect (that furthest from the axis of inflorescence) than on the posterior. At this stage the young flower appears as a short cylindrical body, the free extremity of which is flattened in a direction from above anteriorly, downwards posteriorly (see Plate XXVIII. fig. 2). This very early indication of irregularity is noteworthy, from the circumstance that, as a rule, irregularity commences to show itself only with, or shortly after, the appearance of the appendicular organs.

Calyx.

The sepals make their appearance a little below the obliquely flattened extremity of the floral axis. The two anterior are developed first (Plate XXVIII. fig. 3). Of the lateral sepals and the posterior one, I have not been able satisfactorily to determine the relative time of appearance; but there can be little doubt that the lateral precede the posterior. The sepals soon become connate with each other; but unequally so, the two anterior with each other, and the posterior with the lateral, respectively forming an anterior lip with two lobes, and a posterior with three. These lips are almost free from each other, the antero-lateral connation being very slight. When the sepals are sufficiently developed to cover in the young flower-bud, they are found, in the great majority of cases, so arranged, that the posterior sepal is overlapped by the lateral ones, which are in turn overlapped by the anterior (Plate XXIX. fig. 15). The anterior sepals, as a rule, have not their surfaces in contact.*

Corolla.

The examination of the earliest appearance of the corolla has been the most unsatisfactory part of my research. Its parts very soon become connate, if, indeed, they are not "congenitally" so. I am inclined to think that, as in the calyx, its anterior portion is developed first; the anterior petal appearing to me to be a more salient projection than the others in the early condition. In Plate XXVIII. fig. 4, I have represented a young flower, where the corolla is seen as a rim-like, faintly angular edging to the receptacle, just within or above the calyx, its angles alternating with the sepals. Here the stamens have not yet made their appearance, unless the very slight furrow in the middle line anteriorly be held as indicating, indirectly, the presence of the anterior stamens, one on either side of it. At this stage the centre of the receptacle is seen to exhibit a slight concavity, chiefly in the antero-posterior direction, a concavity which becomes still more marked in the subsequent stages represented in Plate XXVIII. figs. 5 and 6, and which I shall have further occasion to refer to in connection with the development of the pistil. The growth of the corolla appears to continue uninterruptedly until its full development, not exhibiting the pause which occurs so frequently in its course in other plants. As the calyx does not at all keep pace with the corolla, the latter soon forces its way from between the sepals, which at an early period are folded over it; and, in consequence of this, it is only in comparatively young flower-buds that the æstivation of the sepals can be observed. A little before the sepals are thus pushed aside, the spur of the corolla begins to appear, as a small dilatation from within of the tube of the corolla at its base, in the middle line anteriorly, indicated externally by a rounded knob-

---

* Exceptions are sometimes met with. I have seen the posterior sepal overlapping only one of the lateral; or one, or both of the lateral sepals wholly external. A hasty observation of such an exception as the last, probably led PAYER (Leçons, p. 14) to describe the æstivation of the calyx as quincuncial, which I can hardly believe it ever is.

like projection. The process of dilatation or expansion commenced in this portion of the corolla-tube progresses gradually until the period of flowering, by which time the characteristic spur is fully developed. As in the calyx, the connation of the parts of the corolla is unequal in extent, the anterior and lateral petals forming an anterior lip, and the two posterior a posterior one. The æstivation of the corolla is similar to that of the calyx—that is to say, the odd part (here, of course, anterior) is overlapped by the lateral, which are overlapped by the other two parts.

Andrœcium.

In the adult condition, the andrœcium of *Pinguicula* consists of two stamens placed anteriorly. The examination of the flower in its earlier stages, however, reveals the interesting fact of the presence of two lateral rudiments or staminodes. The two fertile stamens appear first—at least they may be seen as distinctly present when the staminodes are as yet very indistinct, if not quite inappreciable. Their appearance seems to follow that of the corolla in quick succession, from the great difficulty I have experienced in finding flowers having the corolla distinctly visible, with at the same time no trace of the stamens. Indeed, even in the stage represented in Plate XXVIII. fig. 4, although the stamens can scarcely be said to be visible, yet, as I have already said, the slight indentation in the middle line anteriorly may possibly be held as indicating, indirectly, the presence of a staminal elevation on either side of it.

The stamens originate as rather large protuberances, which very soon exhibit an oblong figure, being wider from side to side than deep from without inwards. They alternate with the petals, being superposed to the two anterior sepals. In their further development there is nothing very special to be noted. As usual, the anther is formed first, becoming raised upon the subsequently developed filament. The connective forms the great bulk of the young anther, and broadens upwards in such a way that the four anther-cells lie upon its upper surface, what correspond to lateral furrows forming a single transverse one across the top of the anther. Ultimately the anther becomes one-celled, by the occurrence of absorption in the substance of the connective and consequent fusion of the anther-cells. Dehiscence takes place at the transverse furrow just mentioned.

The staminodes originate as mammillæ of small size, compared with the staminal rudiments, and are superposed to the lateral sepals. They are represented in different stages in Plate XXVIII. figs. 5-9. As a rule, they do not proceed beyond the stage represented in fig. 7, and usually become wholly obliterated by the disproportionate development of the neighbouring parts. Sometimes, however, they are developed as shorter or longer styloid processes; and I have met with a good many instances where one or both presented a terminal knob, or were even distinctly antheriferous; in the best developed cases being scarcely distinguishable from the normal stamens. In Plate XXX. fig. 31, I have represented the essential organs of a flower where a moderate degree of this condition is to be seen, accompanied by an interesting reversion to regularity in the stigma, to which I shall afterwards refer.

Pistil.

The pistil appears very quickly after the development of the androecium; it being a matter of some difficulty to find a flower with the staminodes visible that does not, at the same time, exhibit some vestige of the pistil. It makes its first appearance as a semilunar elevation placed anteriorly just within, or (from the downward slope of the receptacle) below the two fertile stamens, with which it alternates. The extremities of this semilunar elevation gradually extend themselves around the organic centre of the receptacle, till they meet in the middle line posteriorly. The ovarian wall, thus completed, grows up as a short tube, which very soon exhibits a tendency to bilabiation, the result of preponderating growth, anteriorly and posteriorly (Plate XXVIII. fig. 9). The orifice of the short tube constituting the young ovarian wall, at first nearly circular, very soon becomes narrowed in the antero-posterior direction. This narrowing, apparently, is mainly caused by the inclination of the anterior and posterior walls towards each other, in consequence of the antero-posterior concavity of the receptacle, to which I have above alluded.* The antero-posterior inclination towards each other of the ovarian walls, is well seen in the sections represented in Plate XXIX. figs. 12 and 13. The anterior and posterior walls thus inclined towards each other, at last come in contact, whereby the cavity of the ovary is closed in above. From this point of contact the lips of the ovarian margin, in their further development, curve away from each other; the one posteriorly as a narrow strap-like body; the other anteriorly as a broadly expanded lamina, which rests upon and ultimately wholly conceals the anthers of the two fertile stamens (Plate XXIX. fig. 11). These lips become covered on their upper surface by papillæ, and together constitute an unequally bilabiate stigma. The part where the ovarian walls are in contact becomes somewhat elongated (apparently to a variable extent), and constitutes the short style. The basal portion of the pistil becomes dilated, forming the ovary proper. It is to be noted that the ovary is to a certain extent inferior posteriorly—that is to say, its cavity posteriorly extends distinctly below the level of the insertion of the calyx and corolla.

Placenta and Ovules.

In the earlier stages of the development of the flower, and up to the time when

* The slight bilabiation of the ovarian orifice seen in Plate XXVIII. fig. 9, though real, is doubtless in appearance considerably exaggerated by this antero-posterior narrowing.

the ovarian wall is completed posteriorly, by the coalescence of the extremities of the original semilunar elevation, the organic centre of the receptacle is somewhat depressed. Almost as soon, however, as the ovarian wall is complete, the receptacular centre enclosed by it begins to be developed as a more or less hemispherical protuberance—the young placenta. At no period of its development has it any connection with the ovarian wall: it is as truly "free-central" as that in Primulaceæ. The ovules make their appearance first on the top of this hemispherical placenta, and continue to appear in succession from above downwards, until the surface is covered by them (Plate XXIX. fig. 16). This placenta does not exhibit the slightest trace of the barren apex, which is so characteristically present in that of Primulaceæ—not even a bare spot,—but is uniformly and densely crowded with ovules over its whole surface. The ovules originate as small mammillæ, which become invested with a single integument, and undergo the anatropal curvature, as represented in the series given in Plate XXIX. figs. 17–22. They are placed so that the raphe is superior where the ovules project horizontally, internal where they have an upward direction, and external where they have a downward one.

Abnormalities.

In the course of the examination of numerous flowers, for the purposes of the foregoing investigation, I have met with a considerable number of cases of abnormality or monstrosity, some of which I think worthy of being recorded.

In Plate XXX. figs. 23 and 24, are represented two cases of remarkable modification in the symmetry. In fig. 23, the flower is dimerous and regular, with two sepals, two petals, and two stamens, in decussate succession. The ovary here is as yet only faintly indicated.* In fig. 24, there are six sepals, of which one is anterior, one is posterior, and four are lateral, these last being conveniently distinguishable as antero-lateral and postero-lateral. Alternating with the sepals are six petals. There are five parts of the androecium, viz., two fertile stamens superposed to the antero-lateral sepals, and three staminodes, of which two are superposed to the postero-lateral sepals, and the third is placed between the two fertile stamens, and thus superposed to the anterior sepal.

The other abnormalities I have figured are some very interesting ones affecting the pistil. In fig. 25, the posterior wall of the ovary is deficient, the placenta and ovules being exposed; the result, doubtless, of imperfect coalescence of the extremities of the primitive semilunar elevation, a defect of development analogous to spina bifida, cleft-palate, hypospadias, &c., in the animal subject. In fig. 26, the posterior (small) lip of the stigma is seen to be bipartite. In this, as in the last abnormality, we have impressed upon us

* This flower was unfortunately detached before I had ascertained whether the sepals were antero-posterior or lateral.

the fact that the posterior middle line of the ovarian wall is a line of suture, and in consequence that the small posterior lip of the stigma is potentially a double organ.* In fig. 27, the posterior lip is normal, but the anterior (large) lip is tripartite. Fig. 28 represents a left† antero-lateral view of the same pistil, showing a slightly marked lobule (*lbl*) at the base of the antero-median lobe; the right antero-lateral fissure, however, was found to be uncomplicated by any such lobule. Fig. 29 exhibits a nearly anterior view of an abnormality very similar to the last; but where a lobule occurs on either side of the base of the middle anterior lobe, that on the left side (to the right hand in the figure) being developed to about the same exent as the corresponding lobule in the last abnormality, while the lobule on the right side is considerably more distinct.‡ I have represented in fig. 30 a pistil with the posterior lip somewhat broader than usual, though undivided, and the anterior lip cleft down the left side, thus exhibiting one antero-lateral fissure.§ A very small notch is seen on the right side, which possibly may be held as representing a right antero-lateral fissure. In fig. 31 is seen an abnormality of quite another character. Here the stigma is altogether undivided and almost quite regular, resembling a funnel the walls of which are to a great extent turned inside out from reflection of the margin. As I previously mentioned, when treating of the androecium, the two staminodes here are well developed, with distinct filaments and anther-like terminal knobs.

Morphological Constitution of the Ovary.

In connection with the monstrous pistils just described, and of course always keeping in view the normal course of development, I would here make a few observations as to the probable morphological constitution of the ovary. The ordinary view has hitherto been, that the ovary in Lentibulariaceæ is bicarpellary, a view supported by the bilabiate stigma, bivalved capsule, and last, not least, by the fact that of the somewhat numerous vascular bundles entering its walls, the two strongest are in the mesial plane, one anteriorly the other posteriorly. This view, however, must be set aside in the face of developmental facts, which show the posterior middle line to be a line of suture. If it be objected that the presence of a strong vascular bundle in the posterior middle line constitutes a difficulty, I need only point to the interpetiolar stipules in *Cinchona*, where we have a well-marked vascular bundle occupying the middle line of the stipule, although that middle line is the line of a suture, and not of a true midrib. There are, it seems

* I have met with three instances of this bipartite condition of the posterior lip.
† To the left of an observer supposed to stand in the axis of inflorescence.
‡ I have in my possession a third example of an ovary with tripartite anterior lip, but as I have been unwilling to remove the stamens from the specimen, I cannot say what appearance is presented on an anterior view; its posterior aspect, however, is almost identical with that given in Plate XXX. fig. 27.
§ This antero-lateral fissure is uncomplicated by any lobule.

to me, only two suppositions possessing any elements of probability and compatible with the history of development: either the ovary consists of one carpel, embracing the extremities of the receptacle; or it consists of five connate carpels, as in Primulaceæ.

With regard to the first supposition it will, I think, be admitted that it is, *à priori*, improbable that a corollifloral plant, like *Pinguicula*, should have only one carpel; all the orders with which it might possibly be compared having compound ovaries. On this ground alone I should be inclined to dismiss the idea.

On the other hand, the 5-carpellary hypothesis has the support of the monstrosities just referred to. In some we have the posterior lip of the stigma bipartite, in others the anterior lip tripartite.* Now, if we combine these monstrosities, we obtain five parts, and these placed in the proper position—*superposed to the petals*. Were we to take the ovary of *Primula*, which originates as an entire annulus, and so modify its development that its anterior part should appear first (just as the anterior part of the calyx in *Pinguicula* appears first), we should have a structure originating in semilunar form exactly as in the young ovary of *Pinguicula*. That five connate carpels should go to form a bilabiate stigma, is just what might be expected in a family where the tendency to bilabiation is so strongly marked. To take an extreme case, I may refer to *Utricularia minor*, where the corolla, with two vascular bundles going to its upper and three to its lower part, is bilabiate with two perfectly entire lips.

General Conclusions.

A few words may be said with regard to the probable affinities of the order Lentibulariaceæ. In the first place, I shall allude to the opinion of Mr BENTHAM, as quoted by LINDLEY (Veget. Kingd. p. 686), to the effect that they are very closely related to Scrophulariaceæ, in "having the same calyx, corolla, stamens, and bivalve capsule, but distinguished solely by their really unilocular fruit, with a free central placenta, and the minuteness of their embryo. In respect of the former character, they come very near to Limosella, Lindernia, and other Gratioleæ, with parallel dissepiments and entire valves; for in these plants the dissepiment is very thin, and usually detaches itself from the valves before maturity, so that being concealed by the seeds, which fill nearly the whole capsule, it often escapes observation, and many of these genera have frequently been described as having a unilocular fruit."

Having, as I think, satisfactorily set aside the idea that the ovary of Lentibulariaceæ is bicarpellary, it is, perhaps, unnecessary on my part to refer to Mr BENTHAM's view, that the premature detachment from the valves of the thin

---

* The variable and inconstant lobules at the base of the middle anterior lobe in this form of monstrosity I am, I think, justified in considering of secondary importance.

discepiments in the Gratioleæ is an indication of an approach to the structure of an ovary with free central placenta; I would only suggest that this is an idea of the same character, and quite as fallacious, as the popular one that the peculiar splitting of the fruit in *Platystemon* indicates an approach in that plant to the apocarpous Ranunculaceæ. If, then, any affinity with Scrophulariaceæ is to be found it must be in the floral envelopes and stamens. In Lentibulariaceæ we have, no doubt, irregular bilabiate floral envelopes and partial suppression of the androecium with a tendency to the didynamous structure; but the value of this combination of bilabiation with didynamy as determining the true affinities of a given plant is seriously open to question. It must, I think, be evident to any one reflecting on the subject, that such a combination of characters occurs in several very different types, by what may be called a parallelism of development or modification. Thus,

1st, In Scrophulariaceæ, with 2-celled ovary and axile placentation; a modification of the Solanaceous type.

2d, In Gesneraceæ and Orobanchaceæ, with 1-celled ovary and parietal placentation; a modification of the Hydrophyllaceous (?) type.

3d, In Labiatæ, with gynobasic style and spuriously multiplied loculi; a modification (in spite of the difference in the position of the raphe) of the Boraginaceous type.

4th, In *Morina* (belonging to the order Dipsacaceæ), where we have a bilabiate corolla of five petals, and four stamens, two large and two small.

On the whole, it seems to me that we have as little right to associate Lentibulariaceæ with Scrophulariaceæ on account of bilabiate floral envelopes and more or less didynamous stamens, as a zoologist would have to associate the Echidna with Hedgehogs or with Porcupines, on account of the remarkable correspondence in their prickly defence.

With regard to the supposed affinity with Primulaceæ, we have a correspondence in what may perhaps be viewed as the most remarkable structure in the Lentibulariaceous flower, viz., the free central placenta; and I have shown at least some plausible grounds for believing the Lentibulariaceous ovary to be composed of five carpels, like that of Primulaceæ. The important differences between the orders may thus be reduced to the position of the stamens and the albuminous or exalbuminous character of the seeds.

PAYER, in his Leçons sur les Fam. Nat. des Plantes, places the order Salvadoraceæ (consisting of the single genus *Salvadora*) in juxta-position with Lentibulariaceæ. Both agree in the superposition of the stamens to the sepals, in having a unilocular ovary with free central or basilar placentation, and in the exalbuminous character of the seed. The question very naturally suggests itself, have we not in *Salvadora*, with oppositi-sepalous stamens and solitary exalbuminous seed,* a plant bearing the same relation to Lentibulariaceæ, with numerous exalbuminous seeds, as Plumbaginaceæ, with oppositi-petalous stamens and solitary albuminous seed, bears to Primulaceæ, with numerous albuminous seeds? I believe that in Salvadoraceæ with Lentibulariaceæ, on the one hand, and Plumbaginaceæ with Primulaceæ, on the other, we have two parallel nearly allied series. I shall not, however, pursue this subject further, as my personal knowledge of *Salvadora* is very limited.

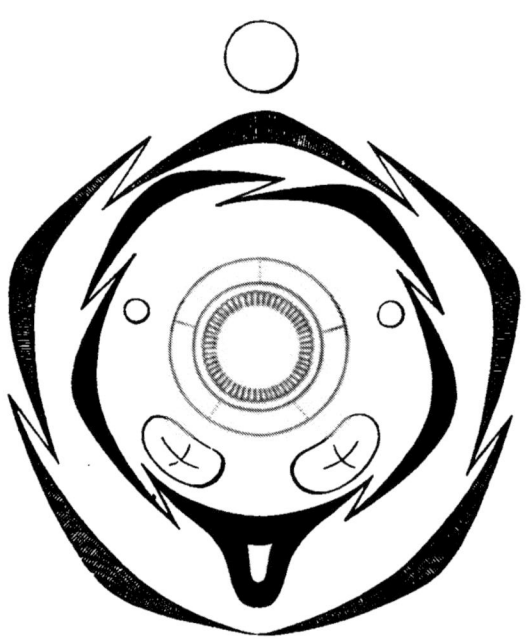

Diagram of the flower of *Pinguicula vulgaris*, L., showing the æstivation of calyx and corolla, the stamens and staminodes superposed to the anterior and lateral sepals, and the one-celled ovary with free central placenta. The wall of the ovary is represented as divided into five parts by two plain and three dotted lines, the two plain lines representing the division of the stigma into two lips or of the capsule into two valves, the three dotted lines representing the abnormal fissures in the above mentioned monstrosities.

* Wight (Icones pl. Ind. Orient. t. 1621), Endlicher (Genera, p. 349), Lindley (Veget. Kingd. p. 652), and Payer (Leçons, p. 14) agree in describing *Salvadora* as having a unilocular ovary with solitary erect ovule. Professor Oliver has kindly examined for me flowers of *S. persica*, L., and *S. Wightiana*, Pl., from the Kew Herbarium, of which he reports in a letter as follows:— "In each of these I find a 1-celled ovary with a solitary basal ovule." My own somewhat limited examination of the flowers of *S. persica* has led me to the same conclusion. On the other hand, Planchon (Sur les Salvadoracées, Ann. des Sc. Nat. 3me serie x. p. 190), and more recently MM. Maout and Decaisne (Traité de Botanique, p. 453) describe the ovary here (Planchon in the genus *Salvadora*, Maout and Decaisne in the order Salvadoraceæ) as bilocular, with two collateral ascending ovules in each cell. The only explanation I can suggest for the statement in the " Traité de Botanique," is that the authors have probably followed Planchon, for M. Decaisne had formerly described *S. oleoides* as having "ovarium . . . uniloculare, loculo uniovulato" (Jacquemont Voyage, p. 140, t. 144); while M. Planchon's description is so opposed to the results of other botanists, and so unlike anything I myself have been able to see, that I am constrained to believe that it was some other plant, and not *Salvadora*, that he examined. I should mention, however, that Decaisne (Jacquemont Voy. t. 144) gives a figure of a fruit of *S. Madurensis* containing three seeds.

Remarks on the Embryos of Pinguicula vulgaris, P. grandiflora, P. lusitanica, P. caudata,* *and* Utricularia minor.

The remarkable diversity in the structure of the embryo in the Lentibulariaceæ is, perhaps, one of the most extraordinary circumstances connected with the order. A. DE ST HILAIRE pointed to the occurrence of a dicotyledonous embryo in *P. lusitanica*, a monocotyledonous one in *P. vulgaris*, and an acotyledonous one in *Utricularia vulgaris*, as an instance of how the most important characters may vary, even within the limits of a single order.†

TREVIRANUS, in 1838,‡ was the first to show that the embryo of *P. vulgaris* has only one cotyledon. In 1848, he published his researches on its germination, which were called forth by a statement of KLOTZSCH's, that this embryo germinates with two cotyledons, of which one is much smaller than the other. Here, he showed that KLOTZSCH's smaller cotyledon does not appear until germination is considerably advanced, thus proving that it does not legitimately fall under the definition of a cotyledon at all.§

P. vulgaris, L. (Plate XXX. figs. 33–40).

The embryo of *Pinguicula vulgaris*, taken as a whole, is of a cylindrical form, with rounded extremities, and measures about $\frac{1}{33}$d of an inch in length. The single cotyledon constitutes about one-half of the entire length of the embryo, and is folded upon itself in a conduplicate manner, its margins being approximate and parallel to each other, except towards the base, where they diverge rather suddenly, leaving a considerable interval, where the termination of the embryonic axis (rudimentary plumule) is to be seen (fig. 33). The apex of the cotyledon is almost constantly entire, or, at least, not sufficiently emarginate to appear distinctly so in a back view, such as is represented in fig. 34. In two, or at most three instances, however, out of the large number of embryos that I have examined, the tip of the cotyledon was somewhat bifid, as is seen in the back view in fig. 35. When sections made in the mesial plane (fig. 38) and at right angles to it (fig. 37) are compared, the rudimentary plumule is seen to be compressed laterally, having a strong convex curvature from side to side, while there is only the slightest possible convexity from before backwards. That there

---

* The observations on the embryo of this species were made after the paper had been submitted to the Society.

† Morphologie, pp. 755–6.

‡ In a communication to a meeting of naturalists, at Freyburg in Br., of which I have seen no report, but which is referred to by TREVIRANUS in his subsequent paper in the Bot. Zeitung, 1848.

§ Botanische Zeitung, 1848, p. 444.

is no trace of a second cotyledon is quite evident from examination of the mesial sections.*

P. grandiflora, Lam. (Plate XXX. figs. 41–42).

After examining the embryo of *P. vulgaris*, I was curious to ascertain whether there was any difference between it and that of this species, which is so nearly allied to *P. vulgaris* that some botanists are disposed to combine them together; and I was gratified to find embryonic characters by which they may readily be distinguished from each other. In front view (fig. 41), the embryo of *P. grandiflora* (which is about the same size as the last) exhibits a single cotyledon having about the same relative length to the whole as that of *P. vulgaris*. The base of the cotyledon, however, is found almost completely to surround the extremity of the embryonic axis, so that hardly a vestige of the plumule is to be seen from the outside; and on back view (fig. 42), the tip of the cotyledon is seen to be constantly and deeply bifid.† The first peculiarity is, so far as I have seen, absolutely distinctive between this embryo and that of *P. vulgaris*; while as to the second one, it is, as I have just mentioned, only in very rare cases that the cotyledon of *P. vulgaris* is bifid at its extremity. These embryonic characters, combined with some other remarkable differences (such as the number of adventitious buds produced at the bases of the outer leaves of the autumn-rosette—in *P. vulgaris*, usually only one in the middle line of each leaf; in *P. grandiflora*, a considerable number in a single transverse row), go far, in my opinion, to establish the validity of the claim of *P. grandiflora* to be ranked as a species.‡

P. lusitanica.

With regard to the very minute embryo of this species (about $\frac{1}{57}$th of an inch in length), I need not say much, beyond confirming the statements of St Hilaire as to there being two cotyledons. These are relatively considerably shorter than the single one of *P. vulgaris* or *P. grandiflora*. I have to note the presence of a trace of albumen in the seed here.

---

* Trevibanus' figure of the embryo from the seed is somewhat faulty, from the cotyledon being represented as considerably too short in proportion to the radicle, and from the absence of any indication of the rudimentary plumule. There is also no indication of the plumule in his figures of the earlier stages of germination, the result, doubtless, of imperfect observation (*loc. cit.* t. iv.). He also makes a curious blunder in describing the apex of the embryo as pointed towards the hilum of the seed (*loc. cit.* p. 442), the fact being that in this, as in all anatropal seeds, the apex of the embryo points away from the hilum, the radicle being directed towards it. This mistake is probably due to the circumstance that there is often a projecting portion of the testa at the chalazal extremity, which is apt to be mistaken for the somewhat similar projection at the hilum.

† I think it not improbable that back views of this embryo may have had something to do with the statement found in most of the books, that there are two "cotyledones brevissimæ" in *Pinguicula*.

‡ I should mention that a very brief statement, by me, of the differences between the embryos of *P. vulgaris* and *P. grandiflora*, has already appeared in the report of a meeting of the Dublin Microscopical Club ("Quarterly Journal of Microscopical Science," viii. pp. 121–2). I now take this opportunity of describing them in greater detail, and with figures.

P. caudata (Plate XXX. figs. 43–44).

Since bringing this paper before the Society, I have succeeded in extracting an embryo, almost entire, from one of a very few seeds of this Mexican species obtained from the University Herbarium in Dublin; and I find that there are two cotyledons, whose length is about one-half of that of the embryo, which measures about $\frac{1}{30}$th of an inch. The embryo here, like the seed containing it, is very narrow and considerably elongated. I have given two views of this specimen, so as to show the division between the cotyledons on either side; from which the fact that there *are* two cotyledons is abundantly manifest. In the specimen figured, one cotyledon is a little shorter than the other; this, however, is accidental, as the cotyledons were of equal length in another embryo which I extracted in a somewhat mutilated condition.

Utricularia minor, L. (Plate XXX. fig. 45.)

The embryo here is somewhat globular, about $\frac{1}{57}$th of an inch in diameter, and at first sight appears to have a smooth undivided surface; on careful inspection, however, a remarkable conformation is to be observed of that end of the embryo which is remote from the hilum of the seed, viz., a minute, slightly convex *punctum vegetationis* surrounded by four slight elevations placed so as to form the somewhat incurved sides of a square. I am not exactly prepared to call these elevations cotyledons; but the whole structure is interesting, as showing this embryo to be a little in advance of a mere "embryonal globule," as are most of the embryos described as "undivided" or "acotyledonous."

Explanation of Plates XXVIII., XXIX., XXX.

Plate XXVIII.

Pinguicula vulgaris.

Fig. 1. Extremity of winter-resting bud, showing rudiment of the inflorescence, and of the axillary bud of the last leaf. l'', 3d last leaf cut across; l', 2d last leaf; l, last leaf; ab, axillary bud of last leaf; fl^1, indication of 1st flower; fl^2, that of 2d flower. Leaf-spiral from right to left of observer supposed to occupy the axis. ×77.

Fig. 2. Young inflorescence further advanced. The first flower (fl^1) distinctly projects, and exhibits irregularity, being flattened from above anteriorly, downwards posteriorly, although not even the calyx has appeared. Leaf-spiral from right to left. ×77.

Fig. 3. Young inflorescence, in which the anterior sepals of the 1st flower are beginning to appear (sa). Leaf-spiral from left to right. ×77.

Fig. 4. Young inflorescence. Here the calyx of the 1st flower is now complete, and the corolla is visible. sl, lateral sepal; sp, posterior sepal. Leaf-spiral from right to left. ×77.

Fig. 5. Young inflorescence. Fertile stamens (st) distinctly present, and staminodes (st') faintly so in the 1st flower. pp, posterior, and pl, lateral petals. Leaf-spiral from left to right. ×77.

Fig. 6. Young flower. Ovary beginning to appear to the anterior side of receptacular centre as a semilunar elevation alternate with the anterior (fertile) stamens. ×77.

Fig. 7. Young flower. The extremities of the semilunar ovarian wall are now extending themselves round the receptacular centre. ×77.

Fig. 8. Young flower. The ovarian wall is now completed by union of the extremities of the semilunar elevation in the middle line posteriorly. The receptacular centre, hitherto depressed, is becoming slightly elevated, forming the rudiment of the free central placenta. ×77.

Fig. 9. Young inflorescence. In the first flower the ovarian wall is completed, and begins to show a tendency to bilabiation. The fertile anthers now show themselves to be 4-celled. Leaf-spiral from right to left. ×77.

Plate XXIX.

Pinguicula vulgaris.

Fig. 10. Young pistil, showing larger or anterior (*a*) and smaller or posterior (*p*) lip of the stigma. The disproportion between the lips is not yet very great. ×85.

Fig. 11.* Young pistil, considerably further advanced, exhibiting nearly its adult form. Anterior lip of stigma broadly expanded, the posterior narrow and strap-shaped. ×15.

Fig. 12. Longitudinal section of young flower at about the stage represented in fig. 9, *pst*, pistil. The placental elevation (*pc*) is now commencing to appear. ×30.

Fig 13. Longitudinal section of young flower at a further advanced stage. The ovarian cavity is becoming somewhat "inferior" posteriorly. As yet no ovules. ×30.

Fig. 14. Longitudinal section of half-mature flower-bud. The corolla now extends beyond the sepals, and its spur (*c*) is of considerable length. The ovarian cavity is now nearly half-inferior posteriorly. ×30.

Fig. 15. Young flower-bud, showing the æstivation of the sepals. ×15.

Fig. 16. Young placenta, showing the basipetal succession of the ovules (*ol*), which have as yet appeared only on its upper part. ×100.

Fig. 17-22. Outline-sections (partly optical) of ovules at different stages of development. Nucleus (*n*); integument (*int*). In fig. 22 the embryo-sac (*es*) appears to have wholly replaced the nucleus.

Plate XXX.

Pinguicula vulgaris.

Fig. 23. Abnormality. Young flower with dimerous symmetry and regular,; 2 sepals (*s*), 2 petals (*p*), 2 stamens (*st*). The ovary is faintly indicated. ×77.

Fig. 24. Abnormality. Young flower with hexamerous symmetry. Sepals—1 anterior (*sa*), 2 antero-lateral (*sal*), 2 postero-lateral (*spl*), and 1 posterior (*sp*). Petals—2 anterior (*pa*), 2 lateral (*pl*), and 2 posterior (*pp*). Two stamens (*st*), here antero-lateral; and three staminodes (*st'*), 1 anterior and 2 postero-lateral. ×77.

Fig. 25. Abnormal young pistil. Ovarian wall deficient posteriorly, exposing the placenta and ovules. *x*, lappet of doubtful significance. ×15.

Fig. 26. Abnormal young pistil, with bipartite posterior lip of the stigma. *a*, anterior lip of stigma; *p' p'*, the halves of the posterior lip. ×85.

Fig. 27. Abnormal young pistil. Anterior lip of stigma tripartite, being divided into an antero-median lobe (*am*), and two antero-lateral lobes, one right (*ral*), the other left (*lal*.) ×85.

Fig. 28. Left antero-lateral view of the same pistil, showing a slightly-marked "lobule" (*lbl*) at the left side of the base of the antero-median lobe. ×85.

---

* In this figure, as also in fig. 31, the capitate hairs scattered over the surface of the ovary are not represented.

Fig. 29. Nearly anterior view of a monstrous pistil resembling the last; but where there is a "lobule" (*lbl*) on each side of the base of the antero-median lobe, that on the right side (to left hand in the fig.) being considerably the larger.   × 85.

Fig. 30. Abnormal pistil. Posterior lip of the stigma (*p*) somewhat broader than usual, but undivided. Anterior lip with a fissure on the left side, separating off a left antero-lateral lobe (*lal*).   × 85.

Fig. 31. Abnormal pistil. Stigma funnel-shaped, and nearly regular. The staminodes (*st'*) here are greatly developed, showing distinct filaments terminated by anther-like knobs.   × 15.

Fig. 32. Monstrous pitcher-like leaf. The dotted line indicates where the cavity of the leaf terminates below.   Natural size.

Fig. 33. Embryo. Front view. Solitary cotyledon (*c*); radicle (*r*); rudimentary plumule or *punctum vegetationis* (*pv*).   × 41.

Fig. 34. Embryo. Back view.   × 41.

Fig. 35. Embryo. Back view, exhibiting an unusual bifid condition of the extremity of the cotyledon.   × 41.

Fig. 36. Embryo. Side view.   × 41.

Fig. 37. Embryo. Longitudinal section at right angles to the mesial plane.   × 41.

Fig. 38. Embryo. Longitudinal section in the mesial plane.   × 41.

Fig. 39. Embryo. Remarkably curved.   × 41.

Fig. 40. Mesial section of embryo similar to the last.   × 41.

Pinguicula grandiflora.

Fig. 41. Embryo. Front view.   × 41.

Fig. 42. Embryo. Back view.   × 41.

Pinguicula caudata.

Fig. 43. and 44. Views from both sides of one embryo, showing the presence of two cotyledons.   × 43.

Utricularia minor.

Fig. 45. Embryo, showing *punctum vegetationis* (*pv*) surrounded by four very slight elevations (*c*) forming the somewhat incurved sides of a square.   × 43.

Trans Roy. Soc. Edin^r Vol. XXV.   Plate XXVIII.

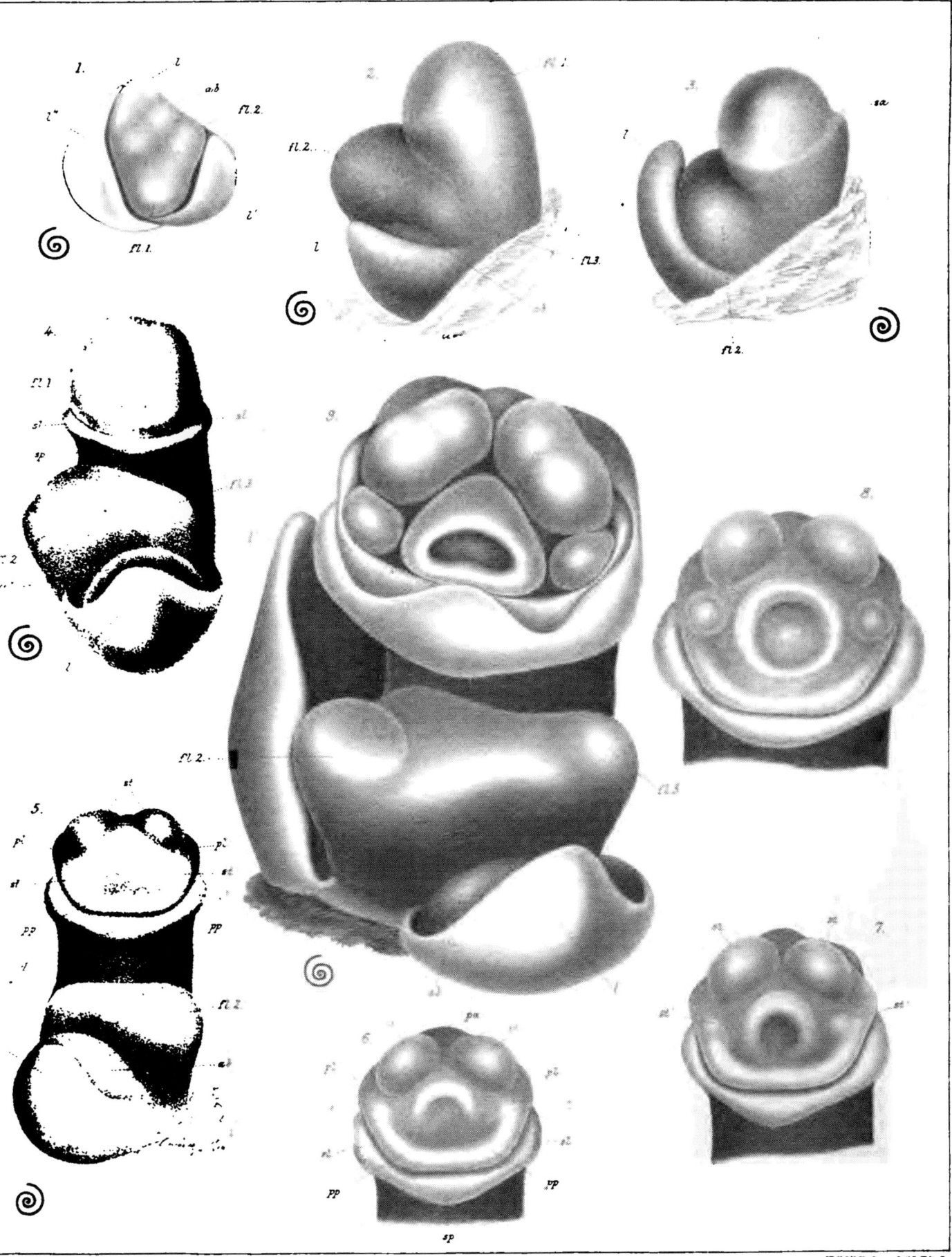

Dickson M.D. del^t   W H McFarlane, Lith^r Edin^r

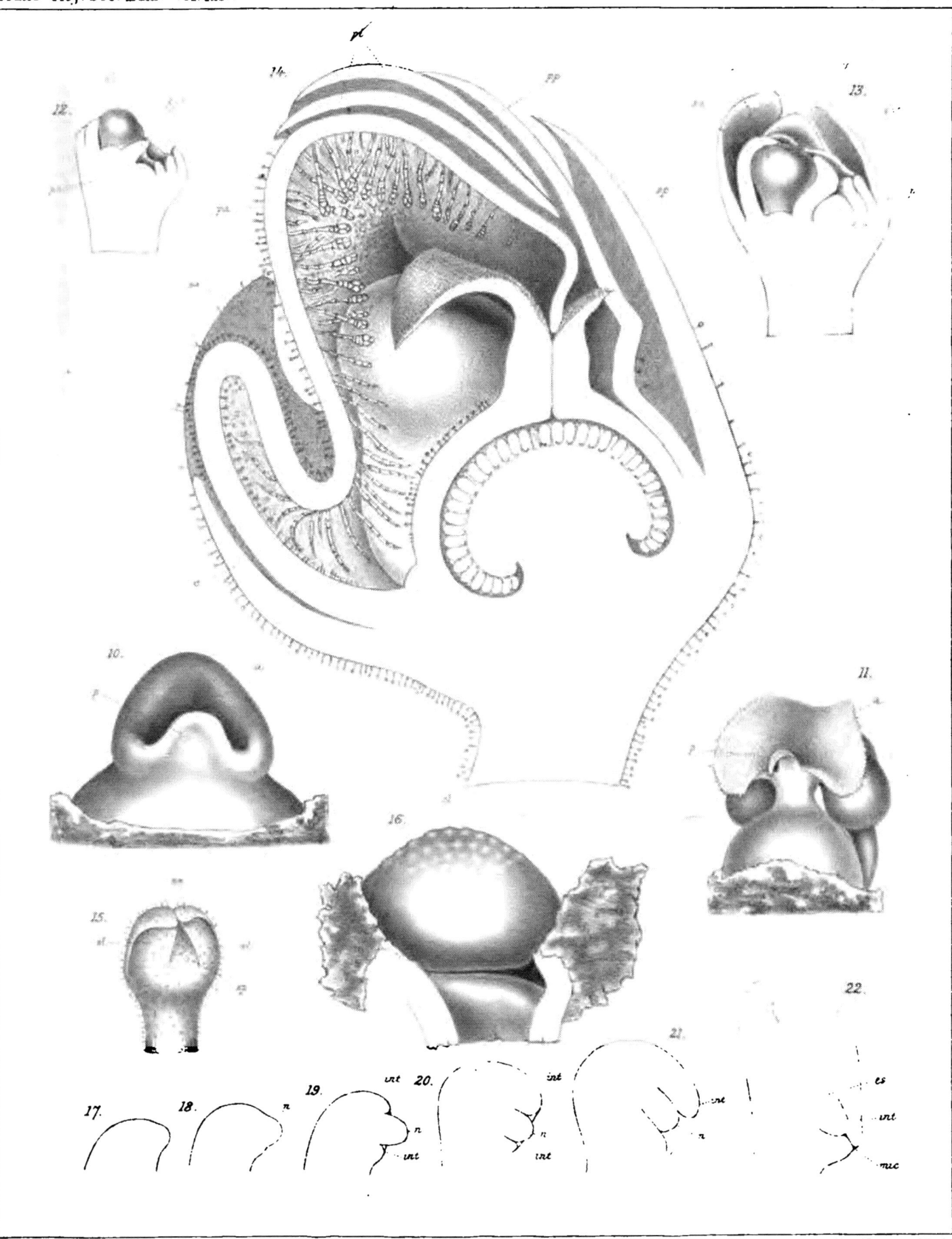

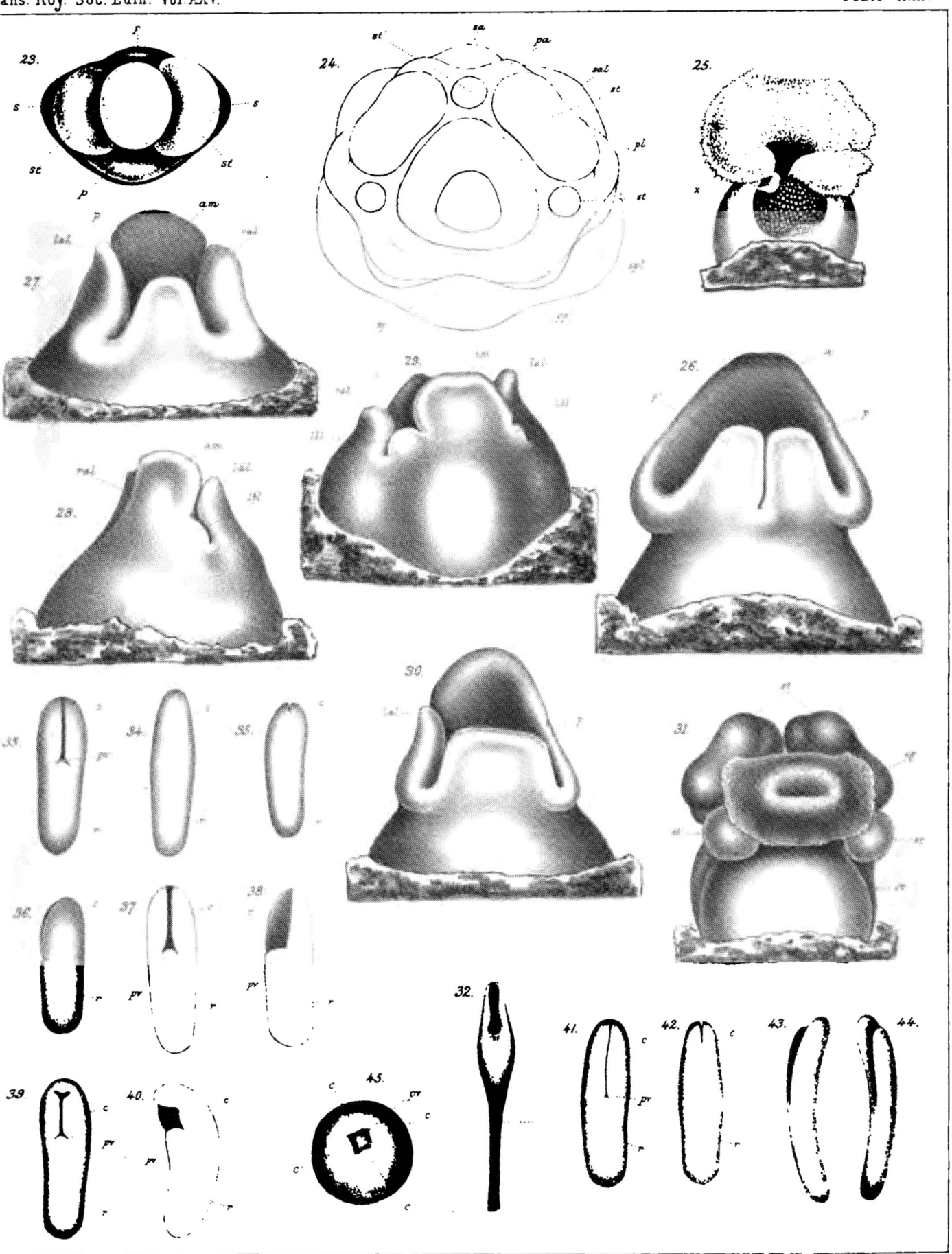